CARDII

DIY CITY GUID JOURNAL

>> CITY NOTEBOOK FOR CARDIFF, WALES

YOUNGHUSBAND EUROPEAN CITY NOTEBOOKS™

ABOUT

THIS CITY NOTEBOOK IS OWNED BY

IF THIS CITY NOTEBOOK IS LOST, PLEASE BE SO KIND AS TO RETURN TO / CONTACT

STARTED

FINISHED

WELCOME TO
CARDIFF
DIY CITY GUIDE AND TRAVEL JOURNAL

This city notebook is designed to inspire listmakers and curators and ingenious travelers to create their own city guide and city biography in list form and to journal the *dickens* out of their time in the city. This city notebooks is a do it (all) yourself notebook crafted for independent travelers and thinkers! So, Cardiff....

Cardiff is a mawr and gwych city! Which begs the question, why not create your own city guide and keep a travel journal to help make your time there unforgettable, fun, and organized, eh?

You hold in your hands a journal and city guide re-invented for listmakers, curators, travelers, urban explorers and city locals alike! This notebook can help you keep all your important information about Cardiff organized and ready for when you need it and where you need it.

Use the pages of this notebook to document your adventures, experiences, thoughts, and memories. Have fun making lists of all the highlights and lowlights Cardiff has to offer. This is the perfect place to journal your time with boots on the ground in Cardiff! This is the perfect place to write down and organize everything you find fascinating about the city — which is why it's your diy city guide.

Make your time in Cardiff more fun, more organized, more productive and more creative by making *Cardiff DIY City Guide and Travel Journal* your newest and trustiest sidekick. Enjoy.

— *Cormac Younghusband*

TABLE OF CONTENTS

GETTING STARTED, 5
Tourism + Transport Info, 6
Emergency Numbers, 6
Personal Information, 7
City Facts + More City Facts, 7-8
You Know You Are From Cardiff When..., 9
When To Visit : What To Bring, 9
The City On The Web, In Books, In Movies, 10

CITY CONFIDENTIAL, 11
Introduction, 12
Claim-to-Fame-O-Matic, 12
Geography & Climate, 13
By The Numbers, 14
Economy, 15
Government, Politics, Media, Faith, 16
Environmentality, 17
Urban Planning, 17
Health, Safety, Scams, 18
City Calendar, 19
City Map, 20
Other City Map, 21
Timeline, 22-23
City Stories, 24
Greatest Scandals, 25
Lures & Snares, 26

CITY FOLKS, 26
Famous & Infamous Sons, Daughters, and Denizens, 27
City Friends and Acquaintances, 28-29

PLACES TO STAY, 30
Places to Stay, 31-32
Camping Grounds & RV Sites, 33

SEE & EXPLORE, 34
Iconic Building & Tucked Away Treasures, 35
Museums & Galleries, 36
Places of Worship, 37
Graveyards, 37
Libraries & Cultural Centers, 38
Neighborhoods & Districts, 39
Famous Streets & Promenades, 40
Parks & Gardens, 41
Flora & Fauna & Animals, 42
Heritage Sites & Monuments, 43
Education, 44
City Tours, 45
Vistas, Views, Zoos, Sanctuaries and Sundry Places of Interest, 46
Offbeat & Quirky, 47
City Walk 1 + Map, 48-49
City Walk 2 + Map, 50-51

EAT, DRINK & BE MERRY, 52
Restaurants, 53
Cafés & Coffee Shops, 54
Bakeries, Pastry, Chocolate, Sweets and Sundry Confectionery Shops, 55
Bars, Wine Bars & Pubs, 56
Nightclubs, 57
Must Try Dishes & Drinks, 58
Best City Recipes, 59

SHOPPING, 60
Flea Markets, Shopping Malls, Bargains, High End Shops Grocery Stores, Antiques, 61-62
Stuff Bought / Souvenirs, 63-64

SPORT, HEALTH AND FITNESS, 65
Places to Exercise, 66
Relaxation & Spas, 67
Spectator Sports, 68

ENTERTAINING STUFF TO DO, 69
Entertaining Stuff To Do (Dancing, Movies, Stage Plays, Music), 70-71

BLACKLIST MUST MISS, 72
Must Not Stay, 73
Must Not See, 74
Must Not Eat : Must Not Drink, 75
Must Not Waste Time Doing, 76
Must Not Waste Money Buying, 77

SPECIAL LISTS, 78
DIY Lists, 79-84

CITY JOURNAL, 85
Journal Pages, 86-135

RATING & EMBETTERMENT, 136
How To Use The City Radar Rating, 137
City Radar Rating, 138
Embetterment, 139

NOTES : SKETCHES : MAPS, 140-144

GETTING STARTED

For every traveller who has any taste of his own, the only useful guidebook will be the one which he himself has written.
— Aldous Huxley

TOURISM + TRANSPORT INFO

TOURIST INFORMATION / OFFICE

TRANSPORTATION : TAXIS, BUSSES

TRANSPORTATION : CAR RENTALS, BIKE RENTALS

TRANSPORTATION : METRO, TRAMS, TRAINS

TRANSPORTATION : AIRPORTS

TRANSPORTATION : FERRIES, WATER TAXIS, BOAT HIRES

EMERGENCY NUMBERS

EMERGENCY : AMBULANCE

EMERGENCY : FIRE

EMERGENCY : POLICE

EMERGENCY : 24 HOUR HEALTH CLINICS

EMERGENCY : 24 HOUR PHARMACIES

EMERGENCY : PERSONAL EMERGENCY CONTACT

PERSONAL INFORMATION

CONTACTS + DOCUMENTS + ID

CITY FACTS

TIME ZONE

TELEPHONE CODES

DEMONYM (WHAT THE LOCALS ARE CALLED)

CITY NICNAME(S)

OFFICIAL WEBSITE

BUSINESS HOURS

CASH MACHINES

BANKING

CURRENCY

MORE CITY FACTS

MAIL & POSTAGE / SHIPPING

TAXES

INTERNET

SMOKING

DOCTORS

DENTISTS

EMBASSIES & CONSULATES

HOUSEHOLD ELECTRICITY

COST OF LIVING

CUP OF COFFEE

HAMBURGER

AIRPORT TO CITY CENTER

NEWSPAPER

FINE WINE

BOTTLE OF WATER

YOU KNOW YOU ARE FROM CARDIFF WHEN....

WHEN TO VISIT : WHAT TO BRING

LIST THE BEST TIMES TO VISIT + WHY

WHAT TO BRING

WHAT NOT TO BRING

THE CITY ON THE WEB, IN BOOKS, IN MOVIES

SITE NAMES + BOOK TITLES + MOVIE NAMES + DETAILS

CITY CONFIDENTIAL

The first requisite to happiness
is to dwell in a famous city.
— Euripides

INTRODUCING CARDIFF

CLAIM-TO-FAME-O-MATIC

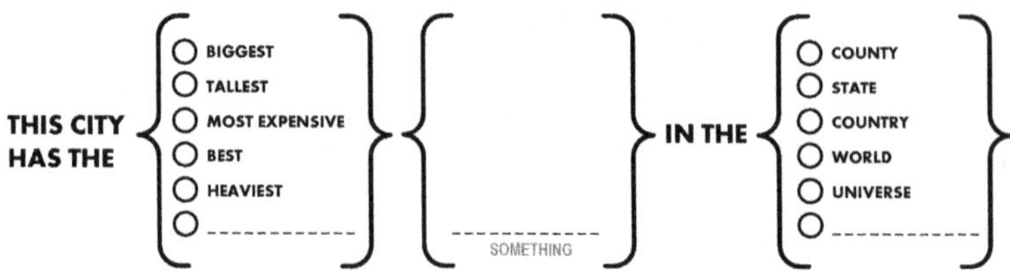

GEOGRAPHY & CLIMATE

REGION

COUNTRY

ELEVATION

COORDINATES

AREA : URBAN

AREA : GREATER

AVERAGE TEMPERATURE

AVERAGE PRECIPITATION

CLIMATE TYPE

- ◯ TROPICAL WET
- ◯ TROPICAL WET & DRY
- ◯ DRY : SEMIARID
- ◯ DRY : ARID
- ◯ MEDITERRANEAN
- ◯ HUMID SUBTROPICAL
- ◯ MARINE
- ◯ HUMID CONTINENTAL
- ◯ SUBARCTIC
- ◯ POLAR

AVERAGE TEMPERATURE

TEMPERATURE

J F M A M J J A S O N D

AVERAGE PRECIPITATION

PRECIPITATION

J F M A M J J A S O N D

BY THE NUMBERS

CITY STATISTICS

POPULATION: CORE	POPULATION: GREATER	POP: % OF COUNTRY	POP DENSITY (KM^2)
POPULATION: % < 15	POPULATION: 15 to 64	POPULATION: > 64	POP: MALE – FEMALE RATIO
TOTAL # HOUSEHOLDS	% HOUSEHOLDS OWNED	% HOUSEHOLDS RENTED	PERSONS PER HOUSEHOLD
AVERAGE HOUSEHOLD INCOME	AVERAGE INFLATION RATE	COUNTRY GDP	CITY % OF COUNTRY GDP
CITY UNEMPLOYMENT RATE	# BUSINESSES / 100,000	AVERAGE INCOME	% LIVING IN POVERTY
MURDERS / 100,000	VIOLENT CRIME / 100,000	POLICE / 100,000	PHYSICIANS / 100,000
INTERNET CONNECTIONS / 100,000	LANDLINES / 100,000	CELL PHONES / 100,000	ADVANCED DEGREES / 100,000
HOSPITAL BEDS / 100,000	FIRE FIGHTERS / 100,000	FIRE RELATED DEATHS / 100,000	HOMELESS / 100,000
CITY BUDGET	BUDGET / CAPITA	CITY DEBT	CITY DEBT / CAPITA
CARS PER CAPITA	GREENHOUSE GAS EMISSION IN TONES PER CAPITA	ROADS PER CAPITA	METRO/RAIL KM / CAPITA
AVERAGE LIFE EXPECTANCY	< 5 CHILD MORTALITY	ELECTRICITY CONSUMPTION PER CAPITA	# ELECTRICITY BROWN-OUT DAYS PER YEAR
% OF WOMEN IN CITY WORKFORCE	% VOTER TURN-OUT LAST CIVIC ELECTION	% OF SLUMS TO TOTAL CITY AREA	% OF POPULATION LIVING IN SLUMS
% POP WITH ACCESS TO POTABLE WATER	% POP WITH WASTE REMOVAL SERVICES	% OF CITY WASTE RECYCLED	GREEN SPACE KM^2 / 100,000

ECONOMY

LIST THE CITY'S MAJOR INDUSTRIES, EXPORTS, AND EMPLOYERS

GOVERNMENT

LIST ELEMENTS OF THE LOCAL GOVT AND CITY SERVICES

MEDIA

LIST THE CITY'S MEDIA PLAYERS

POLITICS

LIST THE CITY'S POLITICIANS AND POLITICAL ISSUES

FAITH

LIST THE FAITHS PRACTICED IN THE CITY

ENVIRONMENTALITY

HOW GREEN IS THE CITY?

LIST THE CITY'S ENVIRONMENTAL CHALLENGES & TRIUMPHS

DESCRIBE THE CITY'S AIR QUALITY

DESCRIBE THE CITY'S WATER QUALITY

DESCRIBE THE CITY'S FOOD QUALITY

HOW GREEN IS THE CITY?

CITY SUSTAINABILITY IS...

- FANTASTIC!
- GREAT
- GOOD
- SATISFACTORY + 1
- SATISFACTORY
- SATISFACTORY - 1
- POOR
- BAD
- TERRIBLE!

URBAN PLANNING

LIST THE URBAN CHALLENGES & PLANS OF THE CITY

HEALTH

WHAT IS IMPORTANT TO KNOW ABOUT PERSONAL AND PUBLIC HEALTH IN THE CITY?

SAFETY

HOW SAFE OR DANGEROUS IS THE CITY? LIST THE WAYS. LIST KNOWN HAZARDS IN THE CITY

SCAMS

LIST COMMON SCAMS IN THE CITY AND HOW TO AVOID THEM

CITY CALENDAR

LIST CITY FAIRS, FESTIVALS, EXHIBITIONS, EVENTS, PARADES, HOLIDAYS AND SUCH

JAN	FEB

MAR	APR

MAY	JUN

JUL	AUG

SEP	OCT

NOV	DEC

CITY MAP

PASTE HERE

OTHER CITY MAP

PASTE HERE

TIMELINE

LIST THE MAJOR HAPPENINGS IN THE CITY (PERSONAL OR HISTORICAL)

TIMELINE

LIST THE MAJOR HAPPENINGS IN THE CITY (PERSONAL OR HISTORICAL)

CITY STORIES

SOME CITIES HAVE SEVERAL MILLION STORIES.
LIST SOME OF THIS CITY'S STORIES

GREATEST SCANDALS

LIST THE GREATEST SCANDALS IN THE CITY'S HISTORY

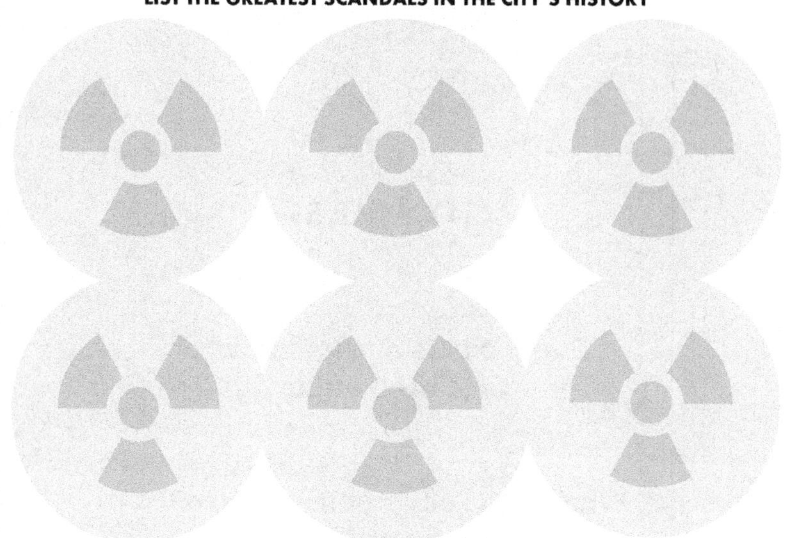

LURES & SNARES

LIST THE TEMPTATIONS & ENTRAPMENTS FOUND IN THE CITY

CITY FOLKS

Every city is a living body.
— St. Augustine

What is the city but the people?
— William Shakespeare

FAMOUS & INFAMOUS SONS, DAUGHTERS, AND DENIZENS

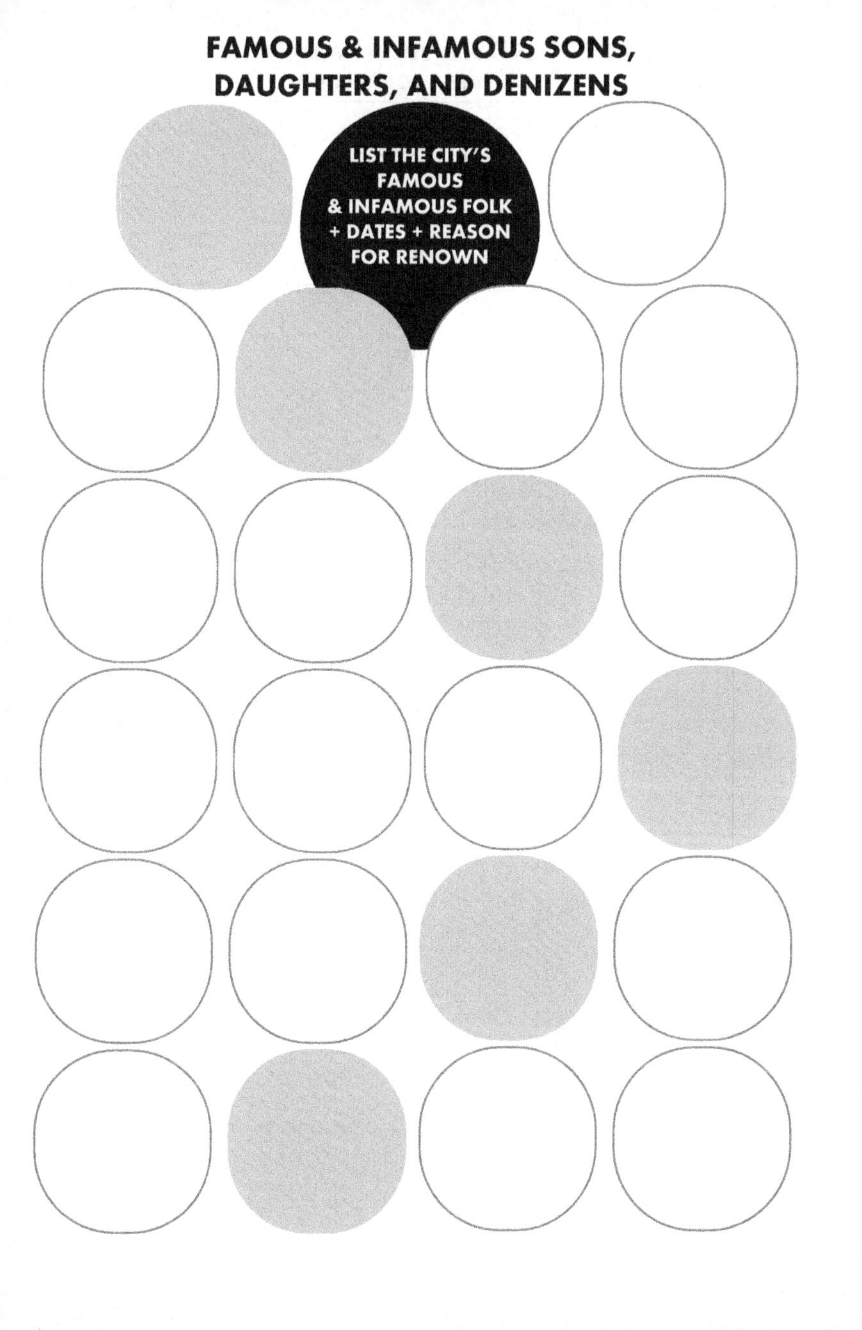

CITY FRIENDS & ACQUAINTANCES

LIST NAMES + CONTACT INFO

CITY FRIENDS & ACQUAINTANCES

LIST NAMES + CONTACT INFO

PLACES TO STAY

To awaken . . . in a strange
town is one of the pleasantest
sensations in the world.
— Freya Stark

PLACES TO STAY

LIST & RATE THE CITY'S MOST NOTABLE PLACES TO STAY

★★★★★

★★★★★

★★★★★

★★★★★

★★★★★

★★★★★

★★★★★

★★★★★

★★★★★

★★★★★

★★★★★

★★★★★

PLACES TO STAY

LIST & RATE THE CITY'S MOST NOTABLE PLACES TO STAY

★★★★★ ★★★★★

★★★★★ ★★★★★

★★★★★ ★★★★★

★★★★★ ★★★★★

★★★★★ ★★★★★

★★★★★ ★★★★★

CAMPING GROUNDS & RV SITES

LIST & RATE THE CITY'S MOST NOTABLE CAMPING GROUNDS & RV SITES

SEE & EXPLORE

I'd like to say "***I've seen it all***,"
but the sights I've seen have
been far too small.
— Cormac Younghusband,
Legendary Nomad

ICONIC BUILDINGS & TUCKED AWAY TREASURES

LIST THE CITY'S ARCHITECTURAL ALL-STARS

MUSEUMS & GALLERIES

LIST THE CITY'S BEST MUSEUMS & GALLERIES + WHEN OPEN

PLACES OF WORSHIP

LIST THE CITY'S NOTABLE PLACES OF WORSHIP (CHURCHES, TEMPLES, ETC) + WHEN OPEN

GRAVEYARDS

LIST THE CITIES GRAVEYARDS, CATACOMBS, AND SUCH + WHEN OPEN

LIBRARIES & CULTURAL CENTRES

LIST THE CITY'S BEST LIBRARIES & CULTURAL CENTRES + HOURS OF OPERATION

NEIGHBORHOODS & DISTRICTS

LIST THE CITY'S NOTABLE NEIGHBORHOODS & DISTRICTS

FAMOUS STREETS & PROMENADES

LIST THE CITY'S FAMOUS STREETS & PROMENADES

PARKS & GARDENS

LIST THE CITY'S BEST PARKS & GARDENS

FLORA & FAUNA & ANIMALS

LIST THE CITY'S MOST INTERESTING FLORA, FAUNA, AND ANIMALS

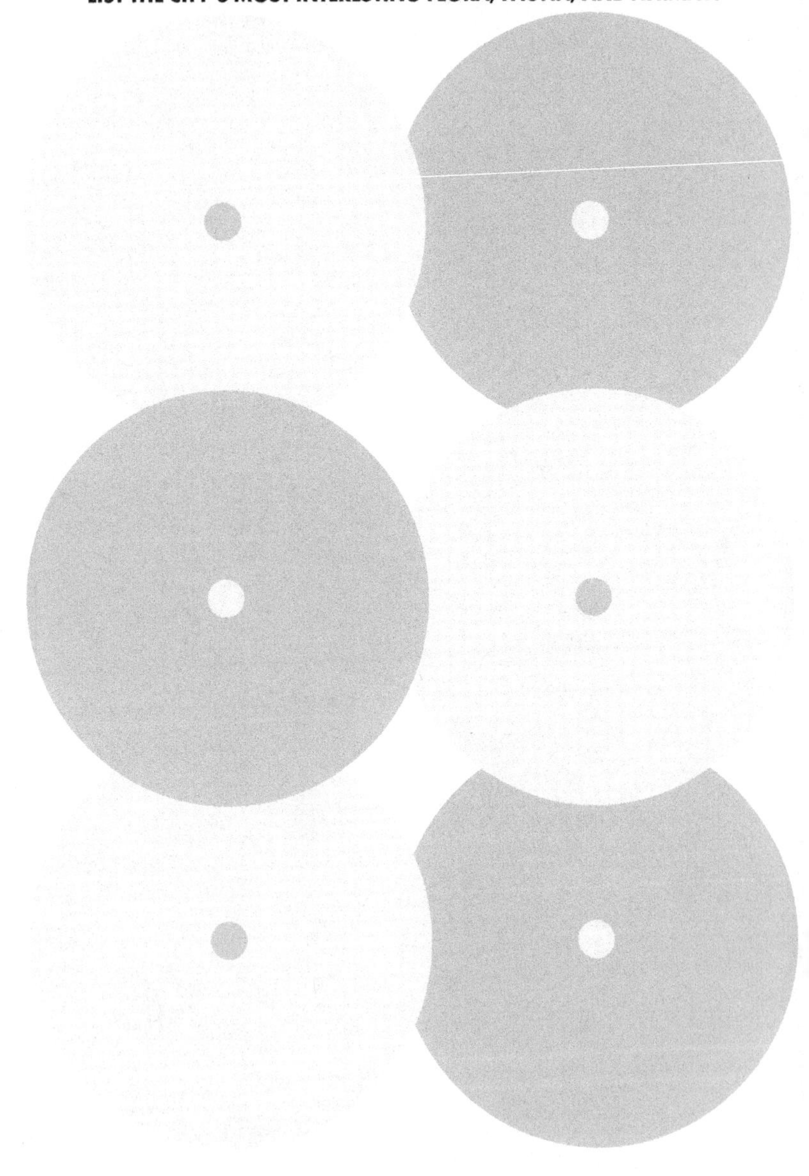

HERITAGE SITES & MONUMENTS

CITY HISTORY: LIST THE CITY'S HERITAGE SITES + ADDRESS + WHEN OPEN

EDUCATION

LIST THE CITY'S BEST UNIVERSITIES, SCHOOLS, AND ACADEMIES

CITY TOURS

LIST NAME + DETAILS OF THE CITY'S BEST TOURS

VISTAS, VIEWS, ZOOS, SANCTUARIES AND SUNDRY PLACES OF INTEREST

LIST THE CITY'S BEST VISTAS, VIEWS AND PLACES OF INTEREST

OFFBEAT & QUIRKY

LIST THE CITY'S MOST OFFBEAT & QUIRKY PLACES

CITY WALKING TOUR 1

NAME OF WALKING TOUR

PLACE	DIRECTIONS	DESCRIPTION

CITY WALKING TOUR 1 MAP

DRAW OR PASTE HERE

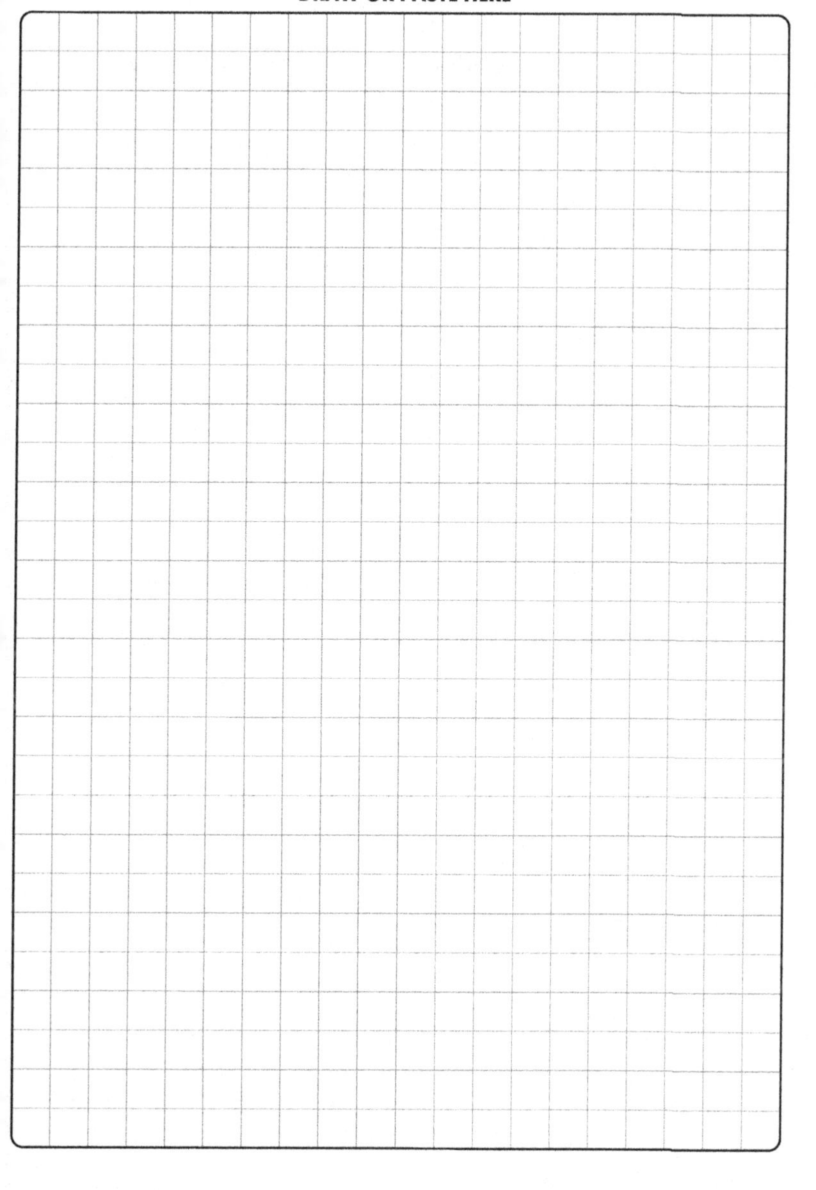

CITY WALKING TOUR 2

NAME OF WALKING TOUR

PLACE	DIRECTIONS	DESCRIPTION

CITY WALKING TOUR 2 MAP

DRAW OR PASTE HERE

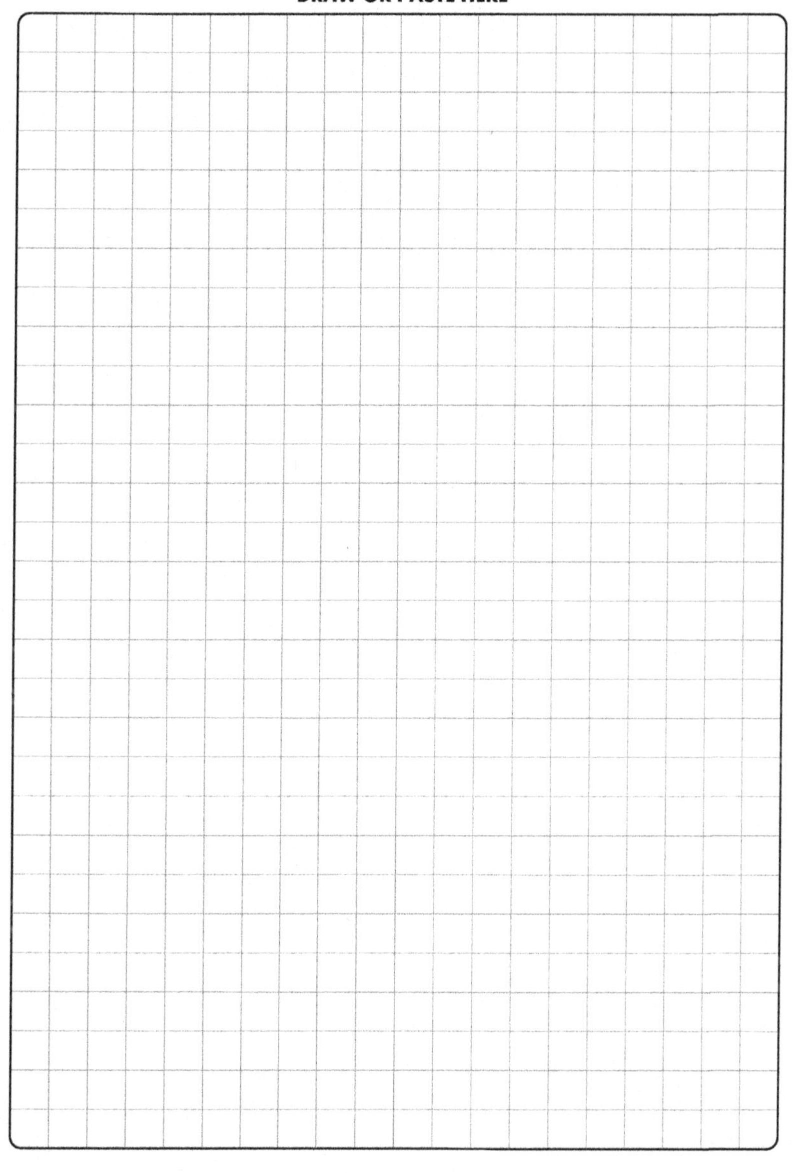

EAT, DRINK, AND BE MERRY

One cannot see the city well,
if one has not dined well.
— Virginia Woolf Misquote

RESTAURANTS

LIST THE CITY'S TOP RESTAURANTS

CAFÉS & COFFEE SHOPS

LIST THE CITY'S TOP 10 CAFÉS & COFFEE SHOPS

BAKERIES, PASTRY, CHOCOLATE, SWEETS AND SUNDRY CONFECTIONERY SHOPS

LIST THE TOP 10 BEST PLACES TO GET DESSERTS

BARS, WINE BARS, AND PUBS

LIST THE CITY'S TOP 10 BARS, WINE BARS, AND PUBS

NIGHTCLUBS

LIST THE CITY'S TOP 10 NIGHTCLUBS & LIVELIEST NIGHTLIFE SPOTS

MUST TRY DISHES & DRINKS

LIST THE TOP 10 DISHES & DRINKS NOT TO MISS IN THE CITY

BEST CITY RECIPES

LIST THE CITY'S BEST RECIPES

SHOPPING

...shopping helped me
discover many new places
and many new things.
— Miuccia Prada

Souvenirs are often looked
down upon as being only so
much worthless gimcrack
and bric-a-brac, yet, as aids
to the conjuring of faded
memory, they can prove
valuable beyond measure.
— Cormac Younghusband

FLEA MARKETS, SHOPPING MALLS, BARGAINS, HIGH END SHOPS, GROCERY STORES, ANTIQUES

LIST THE BEST SHOPPING OPPORTUNITIES IN THE CITY + LOCATION + HOURS

FLEA MARKETS, SHOPPING MALLS, BARGAINS, HIGH END SHOPS, GROCERY STORES, ANTIQUES

LIST THE BEST SHOPPING OPPORTUNITIES IN THE CITY + LOCATION + HOURS

STUFF BOUGHT / SOUVENIRS

THING + CITY PRICE + HOME/ELSEWHERE PRICE

STUFF BOUGHT / SOUVENIRS

THING + CITY PRICE + HOME/ELSEWHERE PRICE

SPORT, HEALTH AND FITNESS

Live in the sunshine. Swim the sea. Drink the wild air.
— Ralph Waldo Emerson

PLACES TO EXERCISE

LIST THE CITY'S TOP GYMS, PLACES TO JOG, SWIM, PLAY TENNIS, GOLF, ETC.

RELAXATION & SPAS

LIST THE CITY'S BEST PLACES TO RELAX AND BE PAMPERED

SPECTATOR SPORTS

LIST THE CITY'S BEST PLACES TO WATCH SPORTS

ENTERTAINING STUFF TO DO

Twenty years from now you
will be more disappointed by
the things that you didn't do
than by the ones you did do.
So throw off the bowlines.
Sail away from the safe
harbor. Go dancing.

— Mark Twain [apocryphal
and misquoted]

ENTERTAINING STUFF TO DO

LIST PLACES TO DANCE, SEE MOVIES,
SEE STAGE PLAYS, CHECK OUT MUSIC, ETC.

ENTERTAINING STUFF TO DO

**LIST PLACES TO DANCE, SEE MOVIES,
SEE STAGE PLAYS, CHECK OUT MUSIC, ETC.**

BLACKLIST MUST MISSES

Hell is a city....
— Percy Shelley

MUST NOT STAY

LIST THE LODGINGS YOU HAVE BLACKLISTED + WHY + RATE USING BLACK MARKS

MUST NOT SEE

LIST THE SIGHTS & ATTRACTIONS YOU HAVE BLACKLISTED + WHY + RATE USING BLACK MARKS

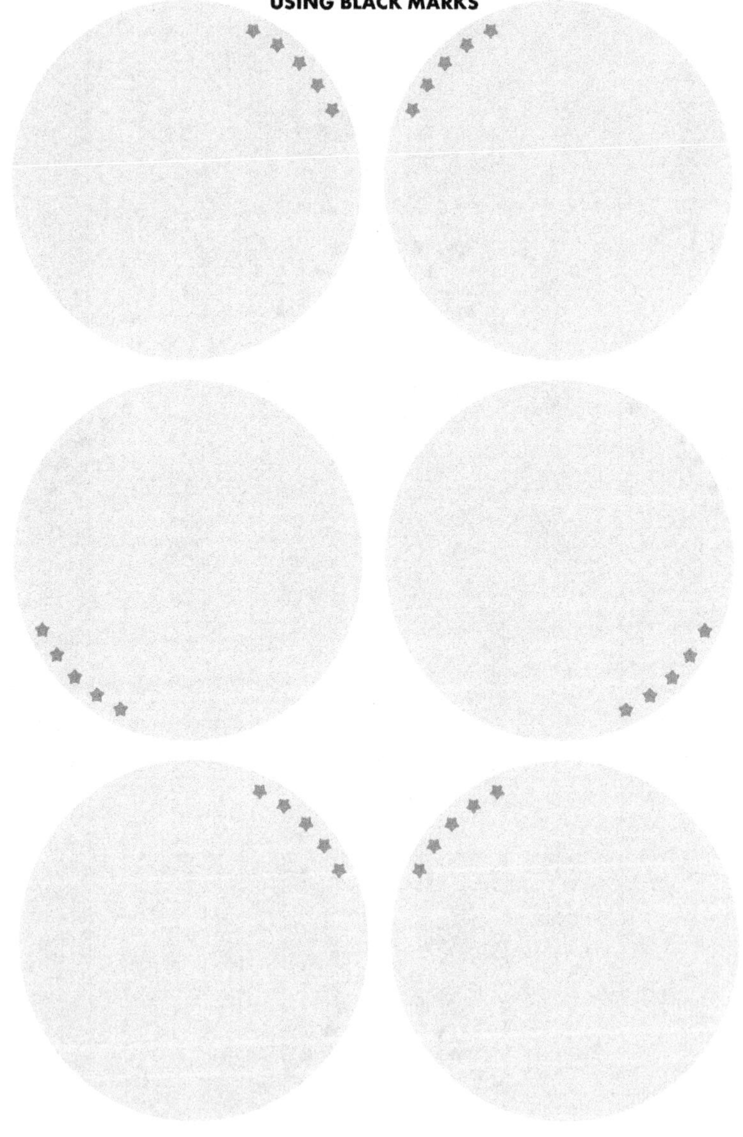

MUST NOT EAT : MUST NOT DRINK

LIST THE FOOD & DRINK YOU HAVE BLACKLISTED + WHY + RATE USING BLACK MARKS

MUST NOT WASTE TIME DOING

LIST THE STUFF TO DO THAT YOU HAVE BLACKLISTED + WHY + RATE USING BLACK MARKS

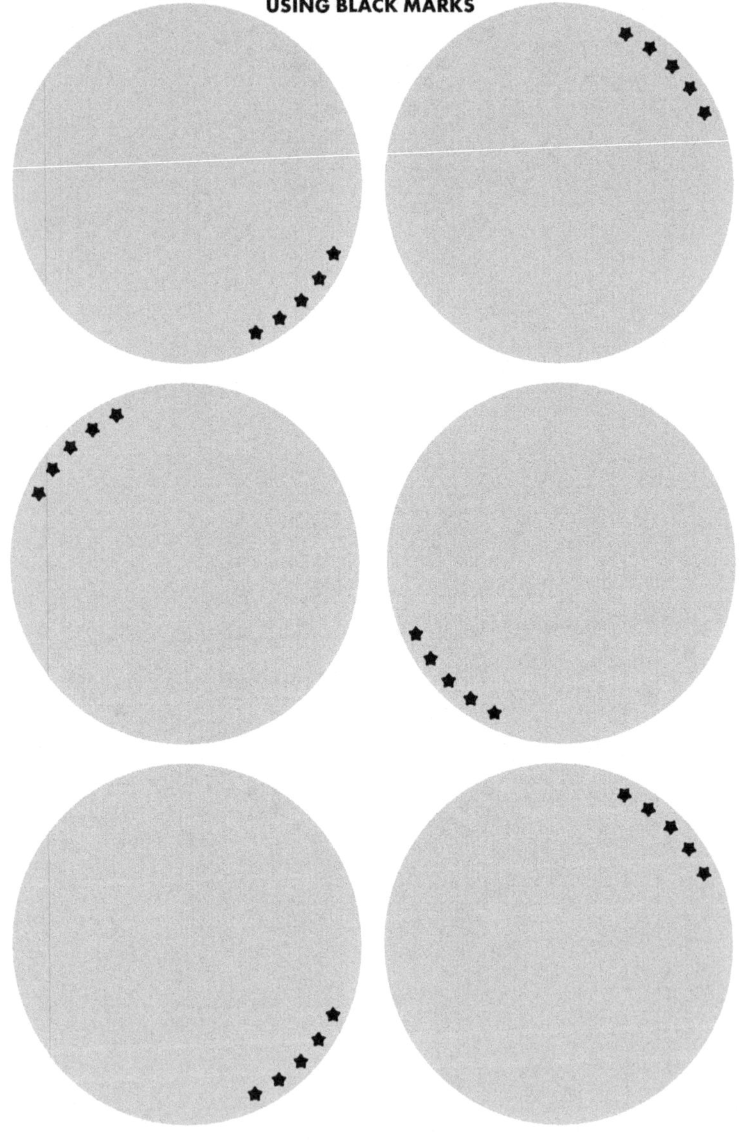

MUST NOT WASTE MONEY BUYING

LIST THE GOODS & SERVICES YOU HAVE BLACKLISTED + WHY + RATE USING BLACK MARKS

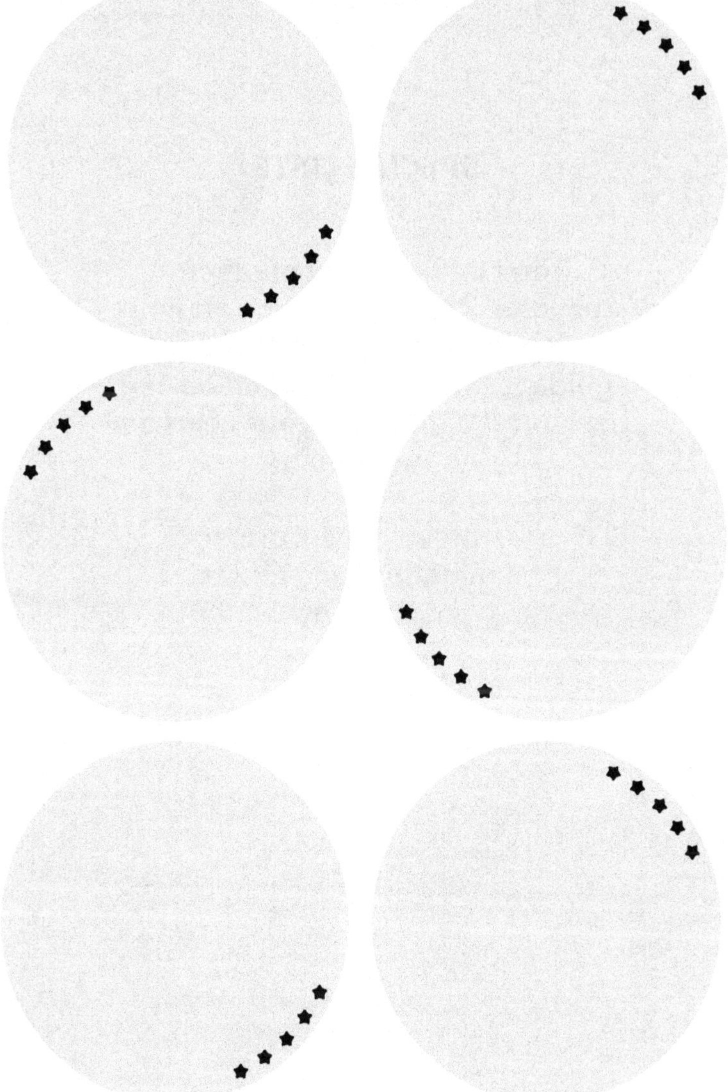

SPECIAL LISTS

Don't let the noise of others' opinions drown out your own inner voice. **This journal and d.i.y. city guide** is, at its heart, about having the courage to follow your heart and intuition.

— Steve Jobs-Cormac Younghusband Quote Mash-up

D.I.Y. LIST

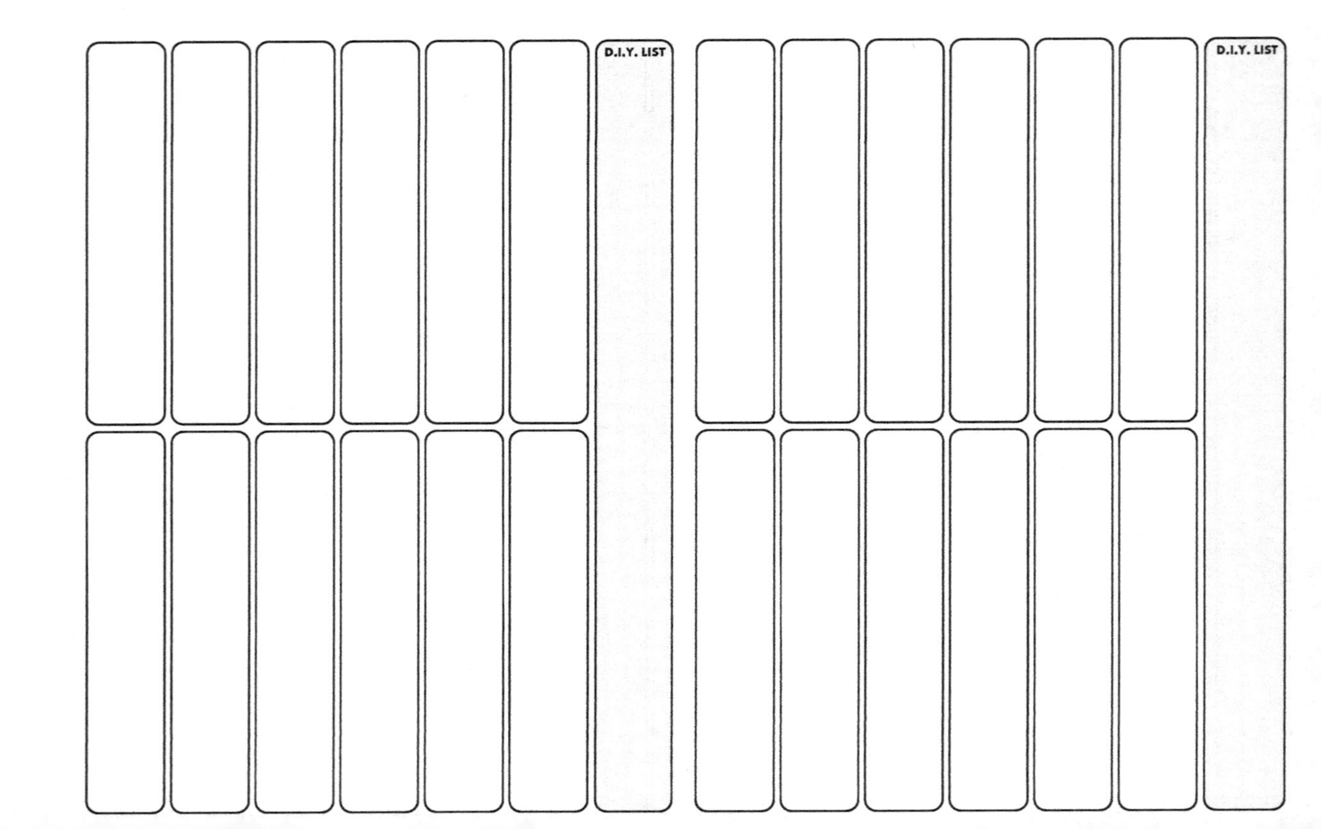
D.I.Y. LIST
D.I.Y. LIST

D.I.Y. LIST

D.I.Y. LIST

D.I.Y. LIST
D.I.Y. LIST

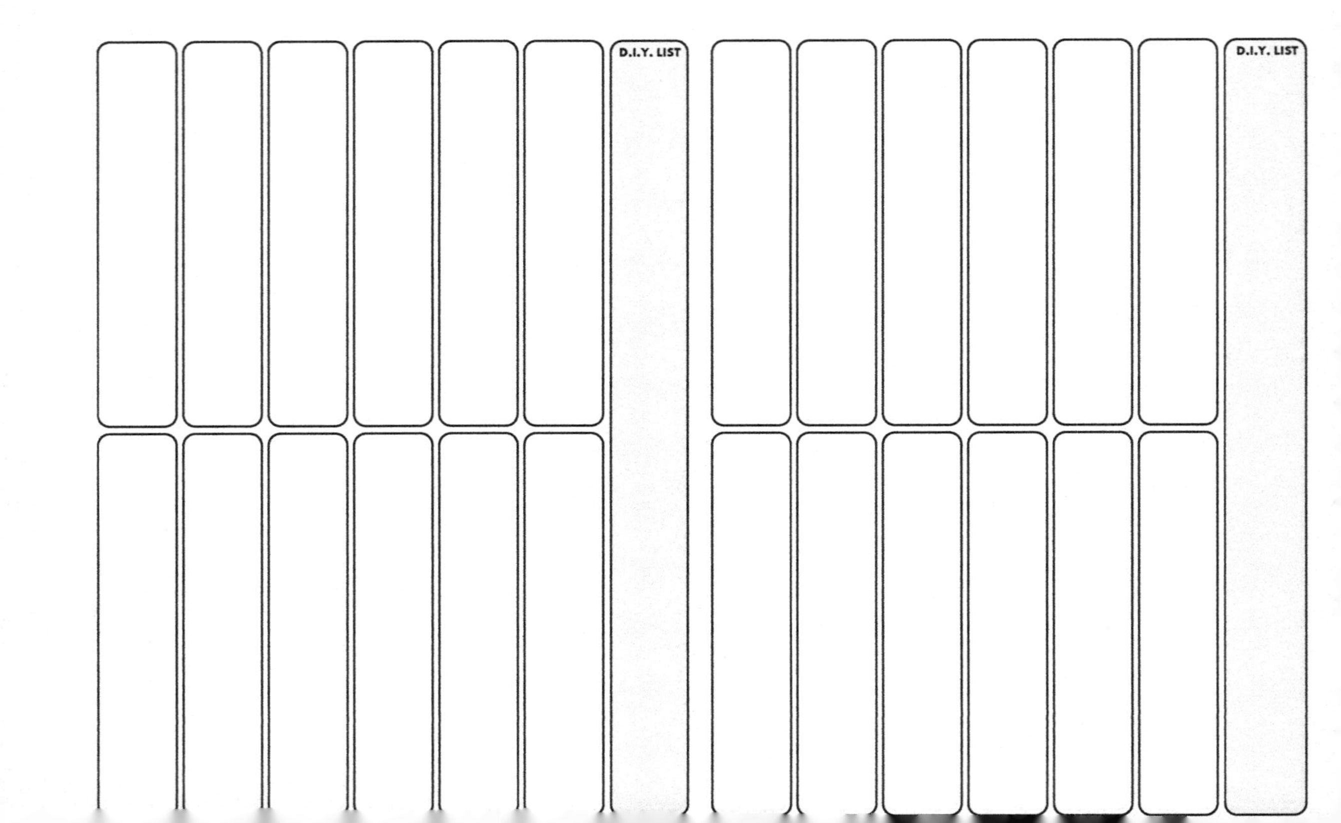
D.I.Y. LIST
D.I.Y. LIST

CITY JOURNAL

In my youth, I assumed all my travel memories would always remain vivid. The sad truth is, all memories fade. Fortunately, memories stick around when we write them down.

— Cormac Younghusband

DAY #

DATE

WIND / RAIN / SKY

TEMP

LOCATION(S)

WHAT HAPPENED TODAY + THOUGHTS ON WHAT HAPPENED

NOTES

HIGHLIGHT OF THE DAY

DAY #

DATE

WIND / RAIN / SKY

TEMP

LOCATION(S)

WHAT HAPPENED TODAY + THOUGHTS ON WHAT HAPPENED

NOTES

HIGHLIGHT OF THE DAY

DAY #

DATE

WIND / RAIN / SKY

TEMP

LOCATION(S)

WHAT HAPPENED TODAY + THOUGHTS ON WHAT HAPPENED

NOTES

HIGHLIGHT OF THE DAY

DAY #

DATE

WIND / RAIN / SKY

TEMP

LOCATION(S)

WHAT HAPPENED TODAY + THOUGHTS ON WHAT HAPPENED

NOTES

HIGHLIGHT OF THE DAY

DAY #

DATE

WIND / RAIN / SKY

TEMP

LOCATION(S)

WHAT HAPPENED TODAY + THOUGHTS ON WHAT HAPPENED

NOTES

HIGHLIGHT OF THE DAY

DAY #

DATE

WIND / RAIN / SKY

TEMP

LOCATION(S)

WHAT HAPPENED TODAY + THOUGHTS ON WHAT HAPPENED

NOTES

HIGHLIGHT OF THE DAY

DAY #

DATE

WIND / RAIN / SKY

TEMP

LOCATION(S)

WHAT HAPPENED TODAY + THOUGHTS ON WHAT HAPPENED

NOTES

HIGHLIGHT OF THE DAY

DAY #

DATE

WIND / RAIN / SKY

TEMP

LOCATION(S)

WHAT HAPPENED TODAY + THOUGHTS ON WHAT HAPPENED

NOTES

HIGHLIGHT OF THE DAY

DAY #

DATE

WIND / RAIN / SKY

TEMP

LOCATION(S)

WHAT HAPPENED TODAY + THOUGHTS ON WHAT HAPPENED

NOTES

HIGHLIGHT OF THE DAY

DAY #

DATE

WIND / RAIN / SKY

TEMP

LOCATION(S)

WHAT HAPPENED TODAY + THOUGHTS ON WHAT HAPPENED

NOTES

HIGHLIGHT OF THE DAY

DAY #

DATE

WIND / RAIN / SKY

TEMP

LOCATION(S)

WHAT HAPPENED TODAY + THOUGHTS ON WHAT HAPPENED

NOTES

HIGHLIGHT OF THE DAY

DAY #

DATE

WIND / RAIN / SKY

TEMP

LOCATION(S)

WHAT HAPPENED TODAY + THOUGHTS ON WHAT HAPPENED

NOTES

HIGHLIGHT OF THE DAY

DAY #

DATE

WIND / RAIN / SKY

TEMP

LOCATION(S)

WHAT HAPPENED TODAY + THOUGHTS ON WHAT HAPPENED

NOTES

HIGHLIGHT OF THE DAY

DAY #

DATE

WIND / RAIN / SKY

TEMP

LOCATION(S)

WHAT HAPPENED TODAY + THOUGHTS ON WHAT HAPPENED

NOTES

HIGHLIGHT OF THE DAY

DAY #

DATE

WIND / RAIN / SKY

TEMP

LOCATION(S)

WHAT HAPPENED TODAY + THOUGHTS ON WHAT HAPPENED

NOTES

HIGHLIGHT OF THE DAY

DAY #

DATE

WIND / RAIN / SKY

TEMP

LOCATION(S)

WHAT HAPPENED TODAY + THOUGHTS ON WHAT HAPPENED

NOTES

HIGHLIGHT OF THE DAY

DAY #

DATE

WIND / RAIN / SKY

TEMP

LOCATION(S)

WHAT HAPPENED TODAY + THOUGHTS ON WHAT HAPPENED

NOTES

HIGHLIGHT OF THE DAY

DAY #	DATE	WIND / RAIN / SKY	TEMP

LOCATION(S)

WHAT HAPPENED TODAY + THOUGHTS ON WHAT HAPPENED

NOTES

HIGHLIGHT OF THE DAY

DAY #

DATE

WIND / RAIN / SKY

TEMP

LOCATION(S)

WHAT HAPPENED TODAY + THOUGHTS ON WHAT HAPPENED

NOTES

HIGHLIGHT OF THE DAY

DAY #

DATE

WIND / RAIN / SKY

TEMP

LOCATION(S)

WHAT HAPPENED TODAY + THOUGHTS ON WHAT HAPPENED

NOTES

HIGHLIGHT OF THE DAY

DAY #

DATE

WIND / RAIN / SKY

TEMP

LOCATION(S)

WHAT HAPPENED TODAY + THOUGHTS ON WHAT HAPPENED

NOTES

HIGHLIGHT OF THE DAY

DAY #

DATE

WIND / RAIN / SKY

TEMP

LOCATION(S)

WHAT HAPPENED TODAY + THOUGHTS ON WHAT HAPPENED

NOTES

HIGHLIGHT OF THE DAY

DAY #

DATE

WIND / RAIN / SKY

TEMP

LOCATION(S)

WHAT HAPPENED TODAY + THOUGHTS ON WHAT HAPPENED

NOTES

HIGHLIGHT OF THE DAY

DAY #

DATE

WIND / RAIN / SKY

TEMP

LOCATION(S)

WHAT HAPPENED TODAY + THOUGHTS ON WHAT HAPPENED

NOTES

HIGHLIGHT OF THE DAY

DAY #

DATE

WIND / RAIN / SKY

TEMP

LOCATION(S)

WHAT HAPPENED TODAY + THOUGHTS ON WHAT HAPPENED

NOTES

HIGHLIGHT OF THE DAY

DAY #

DATE

WIND / RAIN / SKY

TEMP

LOCATION(S)

WHAT HAPPENED TODAY + THOUGHTS ON WHAT HAPPENED

NOTES

HIGHLIGHT OF THE DAY

DAY #

DATE

WIND / RAIN / SKY

TEMP

LOCATION(S)

WHAT HAPPENED TODAY + THOUGHTS ON WHAT HAPPENED

NOTES

HIGHLIGHT OF THE DAY

DAY #

DATE

WIND / RAIN / SKY

TEMP

LOCATION(S)

WHAT HAPPENED TODAY + THOUGHTS ON WHAT HAPPENED

NOTES

HIGHLIGHT OF THE DAY

DAY #

DATE

WIND / RAIN / SKY

TEMP

LOCATION(S)

WHAT HAPPENED TODAY + THOUGHTS ON WHAT HAPPENED

NOTES

HIGHLIGHT OF THE DAY

DAY #

DATE

WIND / RAIN / SKY

TEMP

LOCATION(S)

WHAT HAPPENED TODAY + THOUGHTS ON WHAT HAPPENED

NOTES

HIGHLIGHT OF THE DAY

DAY #

DATE

WIND / RAIN / SKY

TEMP

LOCATION(S)

WHAT HAPPENED TODAY + THOUGHTS ON WHAT HAPPENED

NOTES

HIGHLIGHT OF THE DAY

DAY #

DATE

WIND / RAIN / SKY

TEMP

LOCATION(S)

WHAT HAPPENED TODAY + THOUGHTS ON WHAT HAPPENED

NOTES

HIGHLIGHT OF THE DAY

DAY #

DATE

WIND / RAIN / SKY

TEMP

LOCATION(S)

WHAT HAPPENED TODAY + THOUGHTS ON WHAT HAPPENED

NOTES

HIGHLIGHT OF THE DAY

DAY #

DATE

WIND / RAIN / SKY

TEMP

LOCATION(S)

WHAT HAPPENED TODAY + THOUGHTS ON WHAT HAPPENED

NOTES

HIGHLIGHT OF THE DAY

DAY #

DATE

WIND / RAIN / SKY

TEMP

LOCATION(S)

WHAT HAPPENED TODAY + THOUGHTS ON WHAT HAPPENED

NOTES

HIGHLIGHT OF THE DAY

DAY # | **DATE** | **WIND / RAIN / SKY** | **TEMP**

LOCATION(S)

WHAT HAPPENED TODAY + THOUGHTS ON WHAT HAPPENED

NOTES

HIGHLIGHT OF THE DAY

DAY #

DATE

WIND / RAIN / SKY

TEMP

LOCATION(S)

WHAT HAPPENED TODAY + THOUGHTS ON WHAT HAPPENED

NOTES

HIGHLIGHT OF THE DAY

DAY #

DATE

WIND / RAIN / SKY

TEMP

LOCATION(S)

WHAT HAPPENED TODAY + THOUGHTS ON WHAT HAPPENED

NOTES

HIGHLIGHT OF THE DAY

DAY #

DATE

WIND / RAIN / SKY

TEMP

LOCATION(S)

WHAT HAPPENED TODAY + THOUGHTS ON WHAT HAPPENED

NOTES

HIGHLIGHT OF THE DAY

DAY #

DATE

WIND / RAIN / SKY

TEMP

LOCATION(S)

WHAT HAPPENED TODAY + THOUGHTS ON WHAT HAPPENED

NOTES

HIGHLIGHT OF THE DAY

DAY #

DATE

WIND / RAIN / SKY

TEMP

LOCATION(S)

WHAT HAPPENED TODAY + THOUGHTS ON WHAT HAPPENED

NOTES

HIGHLIGHT OF THE DAY

DAY #

DATE

WIND / RAIN / SKY

TEMP

LOCATION(S)

WHAT HAPPENED TODAY + THOUGHTS ON WHAT HAPPENED

NOTES

HIGHLIGHT OF THE DAY

DAY #

DATE

WIND / RAIN / SKY

TEMP

LOCATION(S)

WHAT HAPPENED TODAY + THOUGHTS ON WHAT HAPPENED

NOTES

HIGHLIGHT OF THE DAY

DAY #

DATE

WIND / RAIN / SKY

TEMP

LOCATION(S)

WHAT HAPPENED TODAY + THOUGHTS ON WHAT HAPPENED

NOTES

HIGHLIGHT OF THE DAY

DAY #

DATE

WIND / RAIN / SKY

TEMP

LOCATION(S)

WHAT HAPPENED TODAY + THOUGHTS ON WHAT HAPPENED

NOTES

HIGHLIGHT OF THE DAY

DAY #

DATE

WIND / RAIN / SKY

TEMP

LOCATION(S)

WHAT HAPPENED TODAY + THOUGHTS ON WHAT HAPPENED

NOTES

HIGHLIGHT OF THE DAY

DAY #

DATE

WIND / RAIN / SKY

TEMP

LOCATION(S)

WHAT HAPPENED TODAY + THOUGHTS ON WHAT HAPPENED

NOTES

HIGHLIGHT OF THE DAY

DAY #

DATE

WIND / RAIN / SKY

TEMP

LOCATION(S)

WHAT HAPPENED TODAY + THOUGHTS ON WHAT HAPPENED

NOTES

HIGHLIGHT OF THE DAY

DAY #

DATE

WIND / RAIN / SKY

TEMP

LOCATION(S)

WHAT HAPPENED TODAY + THOUGHTS ON WHAT HAPPENED

NOTES

HIGHLIGHT OF THE DAY

DAY #

DATE

WIND / RAIN / SKY

TEMP

LOCATION(S)

WHAT HAPPENED TODAY + THOUGHTS ON WHAT HAPPENED

NOTES

HIGHLIGHT OF THE DAY

RATING & EMBETTERMENT

I intend to judge things for myself;
to judge wrongly, I think, is more
honorable than not to judge at all.
— Henry James

With realization of one's
own potential and self-
confidence in one's own
ability, one can build a
better world.
— Dalai Lama

HOW TO USE THE CITY RADAR RATING

Use the **CITY RADAR** to create a signature review of your city. Fill in the radar blips (dots) for each review dimension (and add two of your own). There are four levels for each dimension: excellent, good, fair, and terrible. The blip closest to the outer edge is excellent and closest to the center is terrible. When all the blips are filled in, connect them with a line and shade in the area—the larger the shaded area, the more you liked the city. The result is your own unique signature radar pattern reflecting your overall impression the city. Use this to weigh the good and the bad and clarify your feelings and impressions.

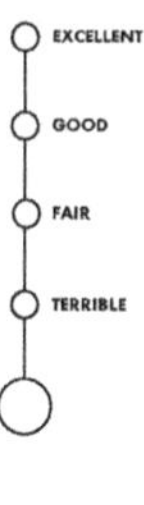

CLIMATE / WEATHER. What did you think about the city's climate?

SCENERY / SIGHTS. What impressions did you have of the scenery / sights of the city?

UNPOLLUTED ENVIRONMENT. Did you find the city clean and fresh or dirty and polluted?

B L A N K (YOU FILL THIS ONE IN). You decide what this one measures. What are you interested in? Golf? Churches? The city dance scene?

FRIENDLINESS / GROSS CITY HAPPINESS. Were the locals friendly? Happy? Or, not so much?

FOOD & DRINK. What did you think of the city's food and drink?

CULTURAL OPPORTUNITIES. Rate you experience with the city's cultural opportunities?

ADVENTURE OPPORTUNITIES. Rate you experience with the city's adventure opportunities?

REST & RELAXATION OPPORTUNITIES. Rate you experience with the city's rest and relaxation opportunities?

INTERESTING / FUN (NOT BORING). Did you find the city interesting and fun? As opposed to boring and dull?

ACCOMMODATIONS. How did you find the places you stayed? Were they up to your standards?

TRANSPORTATION. What did you think of the transportation you took in the city? Was getting around a piece of cake or slice of hell?

COST-OF-LIVING / AFFORDABILITY. How did you find the cost-of-living? Was it an affordable place for you?

SAFETY. Is it safe in the city?

B L A N K (YOU FILL THIS ONE IN). You decide what this one measures. What are you interested in? Beaches? Surf? Beer? Museums? Chocolate?

RE-VISIT WORTHINESS. Is the city re-visit worthy? Do you wish you were there now? Or, are you delighted to have shaken off the dust of this city? Or, if you already live there, is it your fondest wish to keep living there?

CITY RADAR RATING

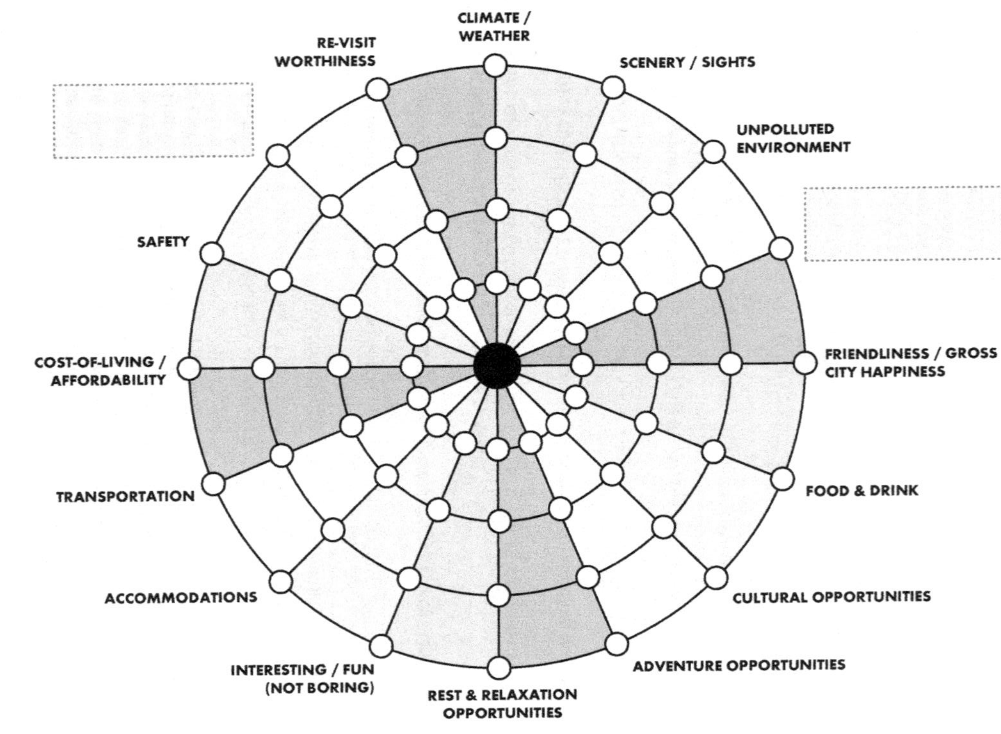

EMBETTERMENT

READ OVER THE RESULTS OF YOUR CITY RADAR RATING AND THEN LIST THE WAYS YOU THINK THE CITY COULD BE IMPROVED

NOTES : SKETCHES : MAPS

NOTES : SKETCHES : MAPS

NOTES : SKETCHES : MAPS

NOTES : SKETCHES : MAPS

NOTES : SKETCHES : MAPS

Made in the USA
Monee, IL
15 May 2022

96470497R00085